Piano

Chop-Monster 1

JAZZ

Shelly Berg

CONTENTS   PAGE

Unit 1	Finding Your Chops	2
Unit 2	Creating Melodies from Chords	4
Unit 3	Discovering Major Seventh Chords	6
Unit 4	Exploring Minor Seventh Chords	8
Unit 5	Playing the Chord Changes	11
Unit 6	Experimenting with Major Scales	12
Unit 7	Advancing with Minor Scales	14
Unit 8	Embellishing with Chromatic Notes	16
Unit 9	Putting It All Together	18
Unit 10	Coming to Terms	19
Unit 11	THAT'S COOL!	20
Unit 12	Learning Dominant Seventh Chords	22
Unit 13	Venturing into Dominant Seventh Scales	24
Unit 14	Understanding the Blues Progression I-IV-V	26
Unit 15	Examining the IV⁷ Chord and the 3rd–to–7th Interchange	28
Unit 16	Feeling the Bluesy 3rd	30
Unit 17	Mastering the Scale for the V⁷ Chord	32
Unit 18	Expanding Your Range	34
Unit 19	Adding More Chromatic Notes	35
Unit 20	Putting It All Together	36
Unit 21	Coming to Terms	37
Unit 22	THAT'S RIGHT!	38

Welcome

As you go through this Chop-Monster book, you will find that improvising jazz is easy and fun, making use of your own inner creativity. Learning to improvise is just like learning to speak. You learned to talk by listening to and imitating your parents, family members and friends. And now you all speak the same language, but you speak it in your own, unique voice.

You will enjoy learning the language of jazz improvisation by listening to and imitating a play-along Compact Disc*. As you listen to the recorded examples, all you have to do is trust your ear. Sing the melodies back, and then find them on your instrument. Soon, these melodies will become your language, and you will be speaking jazz in your own, unique voice. The more you practice the easier and more fun it will be. In the end, you'll be the Chop-Monster!

Have fun!

*Your teacher will play the CD during class. You may also purchase your own CD (sold separately, #251028).

Photography: Elyn F. Marton
Book cover: Students of the Alexander Hamilton High School Jazz Ensemble, Los Angeles, California; Daniel Taguchi, director
    Photographed at The Wherehouse Restaurant, Marina del Rey, California
CD production: Recorded at Stagg Street Studios, Van Nuys, California
    and Sunset Sound Recorders, Hollywood, California

ISBN 0-7390-2941-X (Book)
ISBN 0-7390-3127-9 (Book and CD)

Finding Your Chops

Great jazz improvisers have great **chops**. Your chops are your abilities: tone, technique, and most important for improvisers, the ability to create melodies on the spot. When a musician has the highest abilities (the most chops), the other musicians call him or her a "monster."

❶ SING

Sing the concert B♭ scale, watching your teacher's conducting cues to change to each new note. Your teacher will use the hand signs below. As you sing, say the scale numbers, "One–Two–Three," and so on.

| 1 | 2 | 3 | 4 | 5 | 6 | 7 | 8 |

❷ TRANSCRIBE

Using whole notes, **transcribe** (write down) the concert B♭ scale you just sang.

  1 2 3 4 5 6 7 8

❸ PRACTICE

Follow your teacher's hand signs and **sing** Exercises A and B below.
Once again, say the scale numbers as you sing.

(A)

  1

(B)

④ IMPROVISE

When you speak, you **improvise** (create) each new sentence in a conversation. The **timbre** (sound) of your voice also tells others how you feel. It is the same with music! When you improvise a musical phrase or conversation, you express many different feelings, such as happiness, loneliness, eagerness, sadness, etc.

Ⓐ **Follow** your teacher's hand signs and sing this musical phrase with an *excited* feeling. Begin on B♭.

| 1 | 3 | 1 | 5 | 3 | 1 |

Ⓑ Now follow your teacher closely to **improvise** (create) an ending to the musical sentence.

Improvise!

⑤ RECOGNIZE

Monster musicians work hard to develop "monster ears" by transcribing what they improvise, or transcribing what other musicians sing or play. **Transcribe** the ending you improvised in Line B above. Don't worry about writing the rhythms and bar lines for now; just use whole notes.

CHOP-MONSTER CHALLENGE 1

Ⓐ **Improvise** your own song! Use the scale notes **1**, **2**, **3**, **4** or **5** in any combination. Remember to communicate your music with a specific feeling, such as happy, sad, intense, or relaxed.

Ⓑ **Transcribe** your song below.

Creating Melodies from Chords

The reason that a melody sounds good to us is that the notes in the melody are from the harmony (or chords) of the song. We call these good-sounding melody notes **consonant**. When a melody note doesn't fit with a chord, the sound is not pretty, and it is called **dissonant**.

A chord is several notes stacked on top of each other (or sounded at the same time), creating harmony. *Chords are built in thirds.* This means that if you play *every other note* of a scale, you are playing a chord. If you play the notes 1, 3, 5 of a major scale, you have just played the **major chord** for that scale.

❶ PLAY

Play the notes 1, 3 and 5 of the B♭ major concert scale.

Congratulations! You just played a concert B♭ **major chord** (B♭). If you had tried this with an E♭ major scale, you would have played an E♭ major chord (E♭), and so on. You can see how easy it is to play chords!

❷ TRANSCRIBE

Using whole notes, **transcribe** the notes for the B♭ major chord that you just played.

❸ PRACTICE

When you play up and/or down the notes of a chord, it is called **arpeggiating**, or playing an **arpeggio**. Play the concert B♭ major arpeggio.

❹ IMPROVISE

The CD recording for this series will help you to practice by using **call-and-response** melodies. Call-and-response is a custom where a group leader plays a melody to be repeated, or imitated, by the group.

 Call-and-Response
CD Track 1 has call-and-response melodies for the concert B♭ major chord.

Ⓐ **Practice** singing in response to the melodies. It is important to do your best to *completely* imitate the style and inflection on the CD.

Ⓑ After you are comfortable singing, **play** the melodies in response to the CD.

Try It On Your Own!

Once you are comfortable with the call-and-response melodies from CD Track 2. Track 1, **improvise** your own solo to CD Track 2. Remember, improvising is taking what you already know and expressing it in your own way. So, you can use the melodies you learned from CD Track 1 to play your own improvised solo.

NOTE: *A Compact Disc (CD) is included with the Teacher's Book. Track number references are indicated throughout this book for ease of use if you purchase the CD separately for home use (#251028).*

❺ RECOGNIZE

 Consonant or Dissonant

Ⓐ While listening to CD Track 3, follow your teacher's hand signs and **sing** scale notes **1, 2, 3, 4, 5, 4, 3, 2, 1**. Four of the notes will sound consonant with the major chord, and one note will sound dissonant.

Ⓑ After you sing, **mark with an "X"** in the boxes below the notes that sound consonant and the one note that sounds dissonant.

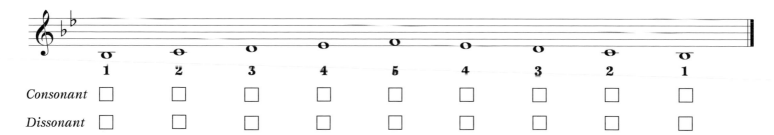

	1	2	3	4	5	4	3	2	1
Consonant	☐	☐	☐	☐	☐	☐	☐	☐	☐
Dissonant	☐	☐	☐	☐	☐	☐	☐	☐	☐

CHOP-MONSTER CHALLENGE 2

Using whole notes, **write** the major chords from the major scales F, E♭, and A♭, using the scale notes 1, 3 and 5. You can choose to arpeggiate or stack the chords. Don't forget the accidentals (sharps or flats)!

Discovering Major Seventh Chords

When you play scale notes 1, 3, 5 and 7 of a major scale, you are playing a major seventh chord. The **major seventh chord** is a very characteristic sound in jazz.

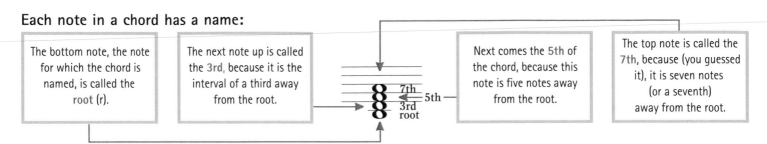

1   2   3   4   5   6   7   8   major 7th chord

Each note in a chord has a name:

| The bottom note, the note for which the chord is named, is called the root (r). | The next note up is called the 3rd, because it is the interval of a third away from the root. | | Next comes the 5th of the chord, because this note is five notes away from the root. | The top note is called the 7th, because (you guessed it), it is seven notes (or a seventh) away from the root. |

7th
5th
3rd
root

❶ PLAY

Play the notes 1, 3 and 5 and 7 of the concert B♭ major scale.

root(r)   **3rd**   **5th**   **7th**

You just played a concert **B♭ major seventh chord** (B♭MA⁷). If you had played 1, 3, 5 and 7 of the E♭ major scale, you would have played an E♭ major seventh chord (E♭MA⁷), and so on.

❷ TRANSCRIBE

Transcribe the notes for the B♭ major seventh chord (B♭MA⁷) that you just played.

B♭MA⁷

❸ PRACTICE

Monster musicians are much like great athletes—they practice their technical "moves" over and over until the process becomes second nature. **Practice** the concert B♭ major seventh arpeggio written below. Play slowly at first, then work up to the monster tempo of mm ♩ = 120!

Ⓐ B♭MA⁷

Ⓑ B♭MA⁷

❹ IMPROVISE

Track 4
Call–and–Response
CD Track 4 has call-and-response arpeggios for the concert B♭ major seventh chord (B♭ MA7).

(A) **Practice** singing in response to the melodies.

(B) After you are comfortable singing, **play** the melodies in response.

Track 2
Try It On Your Own!
Using CD Track 2 again, **play** your own improvised solo. Once again, do your best to incorporate the melodies you learned with CD Track 4 into your solo.

❺ RECOGNIZE

Track 4
Musical Patterns

(A) **Listen** to the first call-and-response pattern on CD Track 4. Note: the pattern is played twice! **Circle** the written pattern that matches:

(B) **Listen** to the second call-and response pattern on CD Track 4. **Circle** the written pattern that matches:

𝒞HOP-MONSTER CHALLENGE 3

Track 5
Consonant and Dissonant
CD Track 5 plays eight examples of chords (2 bars each).

Follow your teacher's cues and play a concert B♭ when you hear each chord. **Mark an "X"** in the boxes below to match whether the note you played sounded consonant or dissonant with the chord.

Example 1	Example 2	Example 3	Example 4
Consonant ☐	Consonant ☐	Consonant ☐	Consonant ☐
Dissonant ☐	Dissonant ☐	Dissonant ☐	Dissonant ☐

Example 5	Example 6	Example 7	Example 8
Consonant ☐	Consonant ☐	Consonant ☐	Consonant ☐
Dissonant ☐	Dissonant ☐	Dissonant ☐	Dissonant ☐

Exploring Minor Seventh Chords

You are going to play a song called "That's Cool!" when you get to page 20. It contains the concert B♭Ma7 chord that you've already learned, plus one new chord—the concert **C minor seventh chord**—that is also found within the concert B♭ major scale.

The concert **C minor seventh chord (CMI⁷)** is simply the chord that starts on the second note of the concert B♭ major scale. In other words, you play scale notes 2, 4, 6 and 8. (It's easy to remember that 8 is the same as 1, up an octave).

chord names: root   3rd   5th   7th   **CMI⁷**

scale notes: 1   2   3   4   5   6   7   8   minor 7th chord

❶ PLAY

(A) **Play** the concert **C minor chord (CMI)**, beginning on the second note of the concert B♭ major scale:

root(r)   3rd   5th

(B) After you are comfortable playing the concert C minor chord, **play** the concert **C minor seventh chord (CMI⁷)**, once again beginning on the *second* note of the scale:

root(r)   3rd   5th   7th

❷ TRANSCRIBE

Label the **root (r)**, **3rd**, **5th** and **7th** of the following major seventh and minor seventh chords:

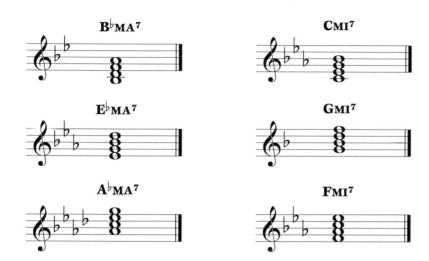

> **IMPORTANT:** *No matter what scale note the chord starts on, the first note of any chord is still called the root (r). So, it's natural to call the other notes in a chord the 3rd, 5th (and 7th).*

❸ PRACTICE

Practice these minor seventh chord exercises over and over, working up to a monster tempo of mm ♩ = 96.

❹ IMPROVISE

Call-and-Response

Track 6

CD Track 6 contains call-and-response melodies for the concert Cᴍɪ⁷ chord.

Ⓐ **Sing** with the call-and-response melodies on the CD. Repeat this track as many times as needed.

Ⓑ After you are comfortable singing, **play** the melodies in response to the CD.

Try It On Your Own!

Track 7

CD Track 7 contains an open track for you to **improvise**. Use your Cᴍɪ⁷ chord and express yourself!

❺ RECOGNIZE

You may not realize it, but you just learned that you can start a chord from the second note of any major scale and build a minor chord, or minor seventh chord. For instance, a G minor seventh chord (GMI⁷) results from playing notes 2, 4, 6 (and 8) of an F major scale. You can learn other minor seventh chords in this same manner.

Ⓐ Circle the second note of each of the following scales to identify the root of each minor seventh chord.

Ⓑ Write the chords in the space provided using stacked whole notes.

Ⓒ Label the root (r), 3rd, 5th and 7th of each chord.

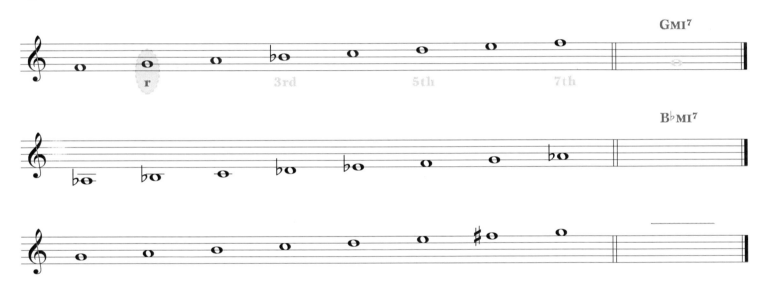

CHOP-MONSTER CHALLENGE 4

Figure out how to play the concert FMI⁷ chord beginning on the second note of the concert E♭ major concert scale. Then, **play** the melodies indicated by the hand signs below.

Ⓐ

Ⓑ

Playing the Chord Changes

❶ GETTING READY

In this unit you will improvise your own melodies to the solo section of "That's Cool!" (measures 36 through 67) where you will find the **chord progression**. A chord progression is the set of chords for a song. Jazz musicians refer to the chord progression as the "chord changes" or more simply, the **changes**.

In the case of "That's Cool!", the chord changes consist of 16 bars of concert C_{MI}^7, followed by 8 bars of $B^\flat_{MA}^7$, and concluding with 8 more bars of C_{MI}^7. You will find that your ear tells you when the song changes from C_{MI}^7 to $B^\flat_{MA}^7$, and vice versa.

C_{MI}^7	$B^\flat_{MA}^7$	C_{MI}^7
16 bars ⟶	8 bars ⟶	8 bars ⟶ ‖

❷ IMPROVISE

Call-and-Response
CD Track 8 will help you improvise convincingly to the song, "That's Cool!"

Ⓐ Once again, **sing** with the call-and-response melodies featured in CD Track 8, listening carefully for when the chords change.

Ⓑ After you are comfortable singing, then **play** the melodies on your instrument. As you sing and play, try to copy the feel and inflection of the recorded examples.

Try It On Your Own!
CD Track 9 is open for you to **improvise** to "That"s Cool!" on your own!

Ⓐ Use the call and response melodies from CD Track 8 as a jumping-off point for your own ideas. Play with a cool attitude.

Ⓑ Practice with this track at least 20 times before moving on to Unit 6!

> **SPEAK THE LANGUAGE:**
> *You have learned part of the jazz language now, so you don't have to speak in "baby-talk" when you improvise. If you play the melodies that you learned with the call-and-response tracks, then you will be speaking the language of jazz.*

CHOP-MONSTER CHALLENGE 5

Monster musicians like to **trade fours** with each other when they improvise. When musicians trade fours, a soloist improvises to the first four measures of the changes, and then another soloist improvises to the next four measures of the changes. The trading continues throughout the progression, with as few as two soloists, or as many as the entire ensemble participating. When musicians trade fours, it sounds like a conversation, because each soloist imitates or expands on the ideas of the preceding soloist.

Trade Fours

Ⓐ With one or more other soloists, take turns improvising four-bar melodies with CD Track 9.

Ⓑ Listen carefully to what each soloist is playing and, when it's your turn, pick up the conversation where the previous soloist leaves off.

xperimenting with Major Scales

When you improvise, scales are another great source for melodic ideas, as long as the chord tones are emphasized enough. As you might have guessed, the concert B♭ major scale is the best choice for improvising to the B♭MA⁷ chord.

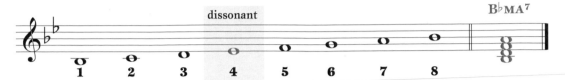

However, with major chords there is one note in the scale to watch out for. The **fourth note** in the scale is **dissonant** against the chord! This means that if you come to rest on the 4th, or skip away from the 4th, it will clash with the chord.

The good news is that it sounds great to go 1/2 step down from the 4th to the 3rd of the chord, and it works to move from the 4th to the 5th. (CD Track 10 will give you a chance to try this out.)

❶ PLAY

Chop-monsters can play any note of a scale at any time! **Play** the notes of the concert B♭ major scale following your teacher's hand signs.

❷ TRANSCRIBE

Improvise a short melody beginning and ending on the root of the concert B♭ MA⁷ chord, using the notes of the scale. Then, **transcribe** what you played.

❸ PRACTICE

Practice the concert B♭ major scale patterns below. Remember to make the eighth notes "swing" like the call-and-response CD.

❹ IMPROVISE

Track 10
Call-and-Response

CD Track 10 contains call-and-response melodies for the concert B♭MA⁷ chord, using the B♭ major scale and emphasizing the chord tones.

(A) **Sing** in response to the melodies. Remember to imitate the style on the CD.

(B) After you are comfortable singing, **play** the melodies in response to the CD.

Track 2
Try It On Your Own!

Go back to CD Track 2 and **improvise** your own solo. Use your B♭ major scale and emphasize the B♭MA⁷ chord tones. Remember to avoid the dissonant scale note 4!

TIP: *Rhythms are also very important to improvisers. Make sure your solo is rhythmic and solidly in tempo.*

❺ RECOGNIZE

Track 10
Matching Melodies

Listen to CD Track 10 and draw lines to **match** the first four melodies that you hear to the written melodies below:

CHOP-MONSTER CHALLENGE 6

(A) **Play** the concert F major scale using the same practice patterns as in the practice section above.

(B) **Try** this Chop-Monster Challenge with other major scales that you know.

Advancing with Minor Scales

In Unit 4 you learned how to play minor chords. You'll remember that the concert CMI7 chord is based on scale notes 2, 4, 6 and 8 of the concert Bb major scale. As a result, the Bb major scale is a perfect choice for the CMI7 chord. In this case, you begin the scale on note 2, which is the chord root.

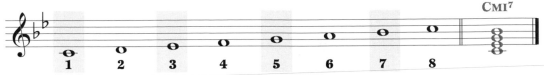

Bb major scale, starting on the chord root C.

With minor seventh chords, all of the notes of the scale are consonant, so the scale can be used without the worry of playing a dissonant note.

❶ PLAY

Play the concert Bb major scale for the concert CMI7 chord, starting on the chord root C.

❷ TRANSCRIBE

 Note Interpretation

Ⓐ Use CD Track 11 and **play** a long tone for each note of the scale to the concert CMI7 chord. Your teacher will conduct each note.

Ⓑ On the staff below, **transcribe** each note that you played. Then, underneath each note, **write down** a feeling that you think each note creates, such as scary, mysterious, strong, bright, etc.

strong

❸ PRACTICE

Practice the scale patterns for your CMI7 chord (your Bb major scale, from C to C).

❹ IMPROVISE

Track 12 **Call-and-Response**
CD Track 12 contains call-and-response melodies for the concert Cmi⁷ chord using the scale and emphasizing the chord tones.

Ⓐ **Sing** in response to the melodies. Remember to imitate the style and inflection on the recording.

Ⓑ After you are comfortable singing, **play** in response to the CD, using your B♭ major scale from C to C. Play along with the track at least five times.

> NOTE: *Musicians often call the minor scale that starts on note 2 of a major scale the* **Dorian** *scale.*

Track 7 **Try It On Your Own!**
Go back to CD Track 7 and improvise your own solo, using the scale patterns you have learned. Remember to think of a mood that you want to create before you play the first note, and carry it through your entire solo.

❺ RECOGNIZE

Track 12 **Matching Rhythm Patterns**
Listen to CD Track 12 and **match** the rhythm patterns written below to the first four melodies that you hear.

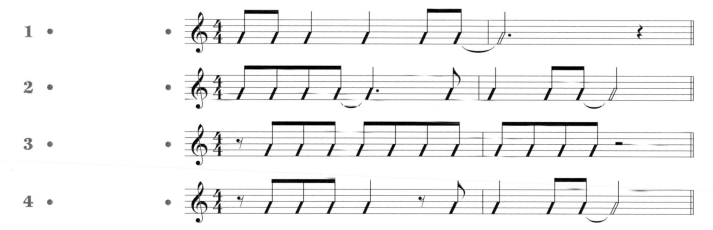

CHOP-MONSTER CHALLENGE 7

By now you've probably figured out that any major seventh chord (MA⁷) will use the major scale of the same name, and any minor seventh chord (MI⁷) can be played with the major scale based one step down. **Play** and **transcribe** the scales for the chords indicated.

E♭MA⁷

FMI⁷

mbellishing with Chromatic Notes

Chromatic notes are notes which are either not in the key you are playing in, or not in the scale of the chord you are playing. So, for instance, any note that isn't in the concert B♭ major scale will be chromatic to the B♭MA⁷ chord.

❶ PLAY

When you are improvising it can sound great to add chromatic tones to embellish the chord tones. For example, you can add the note in-between scale tones 2 and 3 of the concert B♭ major scale. In other words, you will play 2, #2, and 3. Next, you can start on 3 and move down chromatically to 2.

(A) Follow your teacher and the hand signs below as you think of the concert B♭ major scale. The "thumb up" means raise the note chromatically (by ½ step) that you just played. The "thumb down" means lower the note chromatically.

(B) Now think of the Dorian scale to concert CMI⁷. Follow your teacher and the hand signs below and add a chromatic note (½ step) between the 4th and 5th notes of that scale.

❷ TRANSCRIBE

Write the chromatic notes that you played for the scales of your B♭MA⁷ and CMI⁷.

❸ PRACTICE

Practice the patterns below which incorporate the chromatic notes you learned for your B♭MA⁷ and CMI⁷. Remember, all the things you practice can and should be used as ideas for your improvising.

④ IMPROVISE

Call-and-Response

CD Track 13 has call-and-response melodies for the concert B♭MA7 chord, using the chromatic note between the 2nd and 3rd notes of the scale.

(A) **Sing** the call-and-response melodies with CD Track 13.

(B) **Play** the melodies with the CD track until they are easy for you.

Call-and-Response

CD Track 14 has call-and-response melodies for the concert CMI7 chord, using the chromatic pitch between the 4th and 5th notes of that scale.

(A) **Sing** the melodies with CD Track 14.

(B) **Play** the melodies with the CD until they become second nature to you.

Try It On Your Own!

(A) Go back to the open CD Track 9 and **improvise** your own solo, this time embellishing your melodies with the chromatic notes you've just learned.

(B) Try it at least 20 times to make sure the chromatic notes feel very natural.

⑤ RECOGNIZE

(A) Your teacher will play eight different melodies. Four of the melodies will contain chromatic notes.

(B) As you listen, **circle** "Yes" or "No" to identify which melodies contain chromatic notes.

Example 1	Example 2	Example 3	Example 4
Yes	*Yes*	*Yes*	*Yes*
No	*No*	*No*	*No*

Example 5	Example 6	Example 7	Example 8
Yes	*Yes*	*Yes*	*Yes*
No	*No*	*No*	*No*

CHOP-MONSTER CHALLENGE 8

Practice the following chromatic scale until you can play it comfortably from memory.

Putting It All Together

"That's Cool!" gets its name from the **cool** style of jazz, which was played by monster musicians like trumpeter Miles Davis and saxophonists Lester Young and Stan Getz. Cool style playing uses relatively few notes and little or no vibrato.

❶ GETTING READY

Now you are ready to improvise on your own to the changes of "That's Cool!" using *all* of the elements you've learned so far! Once again the chord changes are:

CMI⁷	**B♭MA⁷**	**CMI⁷**
16 bars ⟶	8 bars ⟶	8 bars ⟶

❷ IMPROVISE

Track 15

Call-and-Response

CD Track 15 features call-and-response melodies using scales and chromatic notes.

(A) **Sing** in response to the CD, listening carefully to the style and inflection.

(B) **Play** in response to the CD at least 20 times before trying the next section.

Track 9

Try It On Your Own!

Now **play** with CD Track 9 to improvise to "That's Cool!" using the call-and-response melodies you've learned so far to help form your solo.

CHOP-MONSTER CHALLENGE 9

Monsters listen to other musicians play, not just a little, but a lot! They also transcribe solos from recordings as a way to learn about other musicians' styles. You're going to have a chance to transcribe an entire solo in the cool style, much like Miles Davis would have played.

Developing your transcribing chops will take practice. So, don't be discouraged if this Chop-Monster Challenge takes a while!

Track 16

Transcribe the Solo

Before you begin, it will help you to know that the chord changes are exactly the same as the solo section for "That's Cool!" Plus, every melody is derived from the call-and-response melodies you've already played!

(A) Find some music manuscript paper and a pencil, in case you want to make notes.

(B) **Listen** to CD Track 16 several times through before you transcribe any of it.

(C) **Review** small sections of the solo. Listen and sing to one melody at a time.

(D) **Play** the melodies that you hear, doing your best to get the rhythms right.

(E) Once you think you've got it, play along with the trumpet player on CD Track 16 and see how you did. (You can also play your transcription with CD Track 9 and give it your own interpretation!)

(F) If you can, write down the solo that you have transcribed.

SPEAK IN YOUR BEST VOICE: *Be sure you are listening to yourself, and in the process using your best sound. The melodies you have learned "belong" to you now, and you can be proud to say them, with your own personality.*

Coming to Terms

Write down, in your own words, definitions to these jazz terms:

Consonant: _____

Dissonant: _____

Chord: _____

Major Seventh Chord: _____

Minor Seventh Chord: _____

Root: _____

The "Changes:" _____

Dorian Scale: _____

Chromatic Note: _____

CHOP-MONSTER CHALLENGE 10

Do some research about Miles Davis.

(A) Listen to a recording by Miles Davis and describe his cool style. (One of his most famous cool recordings is a CD called *Kind of Blue.* Listen to the tune "So What." Do you hear similarities to "That's Cool!"?)

(B) What other monster musicians did Miles Davis play with? _____

_____

_____

That's Cool!

Shelly Berg

CHOP-MONSTER CHALLENGE 11

Track 17

Big-Band Recording of "That's Cool!"
Listen to CD Track 17 several times. As you play "That's Cool!," try to imitate the style and articulation of the professional musicians on the recording.

Tips for Jazz Comping (Creating voicings on your own)

1 Playing chords and rhythms is called **comping**. To produce a crisp jazz sound, do not use any sustain pedal (damper pedal). Avoid playing too loudly. Play more of your chords short, rather than long and ringing, and leave plenty of space rhythmically (you don't have to play in every measure). At first, practice playing chords mostly with your *left* hand, and play your chords in this keyboard range:

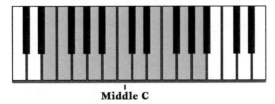

Middle C

2 You can transform triads into jazz seventh chord voicings by lowering the root a ½ step for major chords, and a whole step for minor chords:

3 Now practice comping chords on the "and" of any beat, using short articulation. (Play all examples on this page with your CMI⁷ chord as well.)

 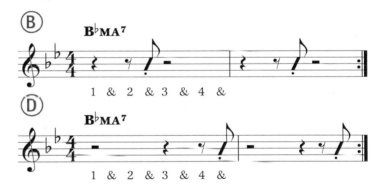

4 Once you feel comfortable with comping off the beat, the next step is to mix up playing chords on the beat and off.

etc.

5 To take a much bigger step ahead, practice comping chords a beat-and-a-half apart, mixing up short and long articulation.

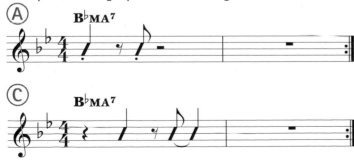 

etc.

Learning Dominant Seventh Chords

You are going to play a song called "That's Right!" when you get to page 38. It contains **dominant seventh chords** which can create a bluesy feeling in jazz music. A dominant seventh chord is similar to a major seventh chord, but the seventh is lowered a ½ step.

So, if you want to play a concert B♭ **dominant seventh chord** (B♭7), you begin by playing the same root, 3rd and 5th that you already know from the concert B♭MA7 chord! The only difference is that the 7th chord tone will be ½ step lower. It is this lowered 7th that gives the dominant chord a more bluesy sound.

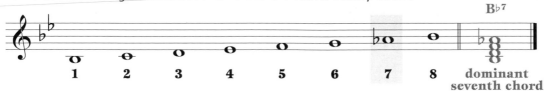

① PLAY

Ⓐ **Follow** the hand signs below to learn the flatted seventh of the concert B♭7 chord:

Ⓑ Next, follow the hand signs below to learn the notes of the concert B♭7 chord. When you see the hand sign for "7," play the flatted (or dominant) seventh of the chord.

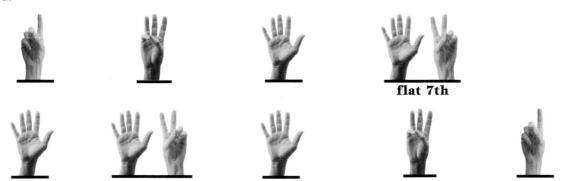

② TRANSCRIBE

On the staff below, **write down** the notes that you just played.

③ PRACTICE

Practice arpeggiating the concert B♭7 chord as indicated below, until you can play it with ease.

Ⓐ

Ⓑ

❹ IMPROVISE

Call-and-Response
CD Track 18 contains call-and-response melodies for the concert B♭7 chord.

Ⓐ **Sing** the B♭7 chord in response to CD Track 18, carefully imitating the rhythms and inflections.

Ⓑ Once you are comfortable singing the figures, **play** with the CD track using your B♭7 chord. By now you should be noticing the *bluesy* inflection that the dominant chord can have.

Try It On Your Own!
CD Track 19 contains an open track for you to improvise. Use your B♭7 chord and express yourself.

NOTE: The call-and-response melodies are short and memorable, and they sound good when they are played a few times in a row. A short and memorable melodic fragment is called a **lick**. *So, now you've learned some pretty cool licks.*

❺ RECOGNIZE

Your teachers will ask for three student volunteers to each improvise a short phrase to the concert B♭7 chord. After each melody is played, **write down** the pitches in their correct order on the staves below. (It's not necessary to notate all of the rhythms just yet).

CHOP-MONSTER CHALLENGE 12

See if you can figure out how to **play**, and then **write down**, the dominant seventh chords that are indicated below.

D♭7   E♭7   F7   B♭7

enturing into Dominant Seventh Scales

Since dominant seventh chords are so similar to major seventh chords, the scales for both are practically the same. All you have to do is play the major scale with a **lowered seventh note** and you can improvise to dominant harmony!

You will discover that, as is the case with major chords, the fourth note of the scale for dominant chords is dissonant, but sounds great when it resolves down to the third note of the scale.

❶ PLAY

Ⓐ **Follow** the hand signs to learn the scale for the concert B♭ dominant seventh chord (B♭7):

flat 7

Ⓑ Next, follow your teacher's hand signs to practice the scale for concert B♭7 in random note order.

❷ TRANSCRIBE

Your teacher will display a series of hand signs to the scale for B♭7. As each hand sign is displayed, **write down** its pitch on the staff below:

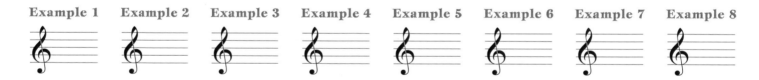

| Example 1 | Example 2 | Example 3 | Example 4 | Example 5 | Example 6 | Example 7 | Example 8 |

❸ PRACTICE

Practice the scale for the concert B♭7 chord as indicated below, until you can execute the patterns with ease and fluidity.

❹ IMPROVISE

Track 20

Call-and-Response

CD Track 20 has call-and-response patterns for the scale to concert Bb⁷.

(A) **Practice** singing the melodies, carefully imitating inflections and rhythms.

(B) Once you are comfortable singing the melodies, **play** in response to the CD.

(C) Play along with the track five more times and think about which melodic phrase you liked the most. Describe why it was your favorite: _____

> *NOTE: Some jazz musicians refer to the scale for dominant chords by its modal name, **Mixolydian**.*

❺ RECOGNIZE

Track 21

Chord Matching

CD Track 21 will play a series of eight chords with their scales.

Mark with an "X" whether each chord is a **dominant** seventh chord or a **major** seventh chord. (Remember to listen for the bluesy 7th.)

Example 1	Example 2	Example 3	Example 4
Dominant 7th ☐	*Dominant 7th* ☐	*Dominant 7th* ☐	*Dominant 7th* ☐
Major 7th ☐	*Major 7th* ☐	*Major 7th* ☐	*Major 7th* ☐

Example 5	Example 6	Example 7	Example 8
Dominant 7th ☐	*Dominant 7th* ☐	*Dominant 7th* ☐	*Dominant 7th* ☐
Major 7th ☐	*Major 7th* ☐	*Major 7th* ☐	*Major 7th* ☐

𝒞HOP-MONSTER CHALLENGE 13

See if you can **play** and **transcribe** the scales to the dominant seventh chords below:

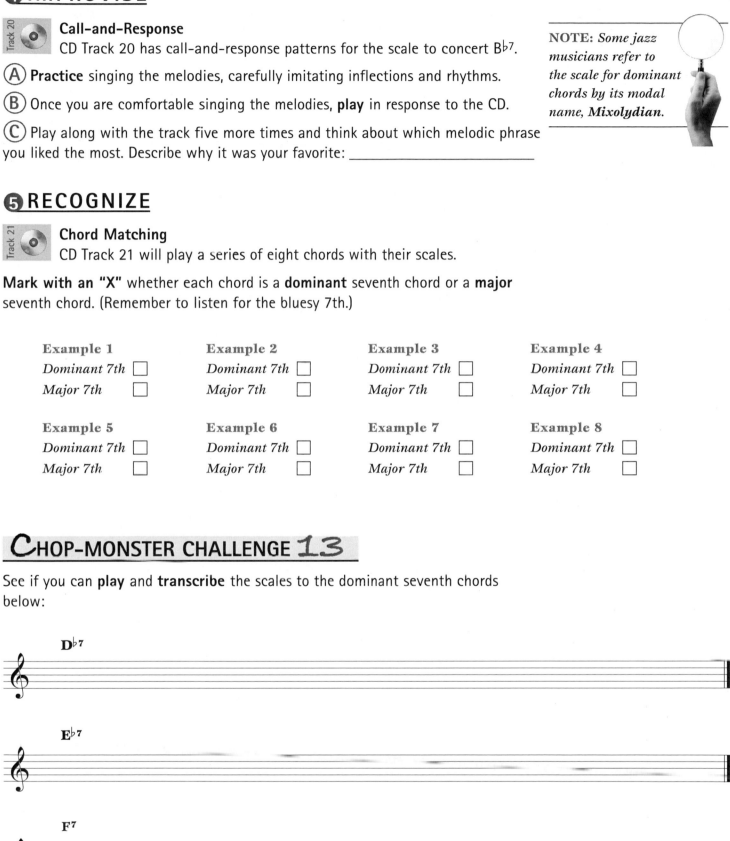

D♭⁷

E♭⁷

F⁷

Understanding the Blues Progression I-IV-V

The **12-bar blues** is a chord progression that finds its origins in the field songs of American slavery. It is the most commonly played progression in jazz and there are thousands of *blues heads* (melodies written to blues changes). The **head** is what jazz musicians call the melody of a song.

In its simplest form, the 12-bar blues is based on just three dominant chords. These chords are built on the 1st, 4th and 5th notes of the scale. A chord built on the first note of the scale is called the **One chord (I)**, or also the **Tonic chord**. So, in the key of concert B♭, the Tonic (I) chord is a B♭ chord.

A chord built over the fourth note of the scale is called the **Four chord (IV)** and a chord built upon the fifth note of the scale is, you guessed it, the **Five chord (V)**.

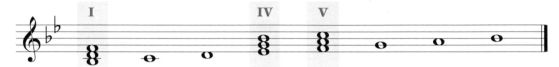

Good news! You can play the blues based on your knowledge of the Tonic chord, which you already know. You will learn about the IV and V chords later on in this book.

So here is the basic blues progression. It begins with four bars of the Tonic chord (I).

I
4 bars ——————————————————————————————→ |

Next are two bars of the IV chord, returning back to two more bars of the I chord.

IV | **I**
2 bars ——————————→ | 2 bars ——————————→ |

The last four bars are divided into two bars of the V chord and a final two bars of the I chord, as show below.

V | **I**
2 bars ——————————→ | 2 bars ——————————→ ‖

❶ SING

12-Bar Blues Progression
CD Track 22 features the chord roots of the 12-bar blues progression.
Practice singing and then playing along. This is NOT a call-and-response track: you simply sing or play along. Practice until the roots are memorized and second nature to you. Begin on your B♭ chord, (the I chord).

❷ TRANSCRIBE

On the staff below, **write down** the roots of the I, IV and V chords for the B♭ blues progression as indicated, and the first three notes of a scale for each root. This will be easy, because all of the notes you need are in the concert B♭ scale.

❸ PRACTICE

Practice the 3-note scales that you just wrote as indicated on the staves below. This will help you get more comfortable playing and hearing around the roots of the chords for the 12-bar blues changes.

❹ IMPROVISE

Call-and-Response
CD Track 23 has call-and-response melodies featuring the 3-note scales you have been practicing above. After you are comfortably **singing** in response to the CD, practice **playing** the response patterns. **Congratulations!** You are improvising to the 12-bar blues!

> **IMPORTANT:** *Learning to play the blues is an essential element in building your chops and mastering the jazz language.*

❺ RECOGNIZE

Recognizing Chord Roots
CD Track 24 is NOT a call-and-response track. In this instance the track features a progression that is NOT the blues, but is made up of I, IV and V chords. **Write down** the Roman numeral names and chord roots each time you hear the chord change, as played by the trumpet player.

	Example 1	Example 2	Example 3	Example 4	Example 5	Example 6	Example 7	Example 8
Roman numerals								
Chord roots:								

CHOP-MONSTER CHALLENGE 14

I, IV and V Chords
This Chop-Monster Challenge is similar to the Recognize exercise above, but on CD Track 25 there is no trumpet to help you hear the chord roots. Monster jazz musicians can identify chord changes by listening just to the bass and piano.

	Example 1	Example 2	Example 3	Example 4	Example 5	Example 6	Example 7	Example 8
Roman numerals								
Chord roots:								

xamining the IV⁷ Chord and The 3rd-to-7th Interchange

By now you should know that the root of the **IV chord** in the concert key of B♭ major is E♭.

The only other thing you need to know before improvising to the IV chord is that there is only **one note** that changes for the scale, as compared to playing the scale for I⁷. You can simply take the scale that you played for the B♭⁷, then **lower the third note of the scale a ½ step**, and you will be playing all of the right notes for your E♭⁷ chord. It's amazing how easy that is!

PLAY

(A) As a **review**, follow the hand signs below to play the scale you already know for the concert B♭⁷ chord. Remember to play the lowered 7th note.

(B) Next, follow the hand signs below to play the notes of the scale for the IV⁷ chord (E♭⁷). Remember that the only note that changes is the third note, which will be a ½ step lower.

TRANSCRIBE

(A) Write down the scale for B♭⁷ (the I⁷ chord in concert B♭ blues).

I⁷

(B) Now write down the scale tones for your E♭⁷ that you played to the hand signs in Line B above. Circle the third note of each scale. You should notice that the circled notes are the only different notes in the two scales.

IV⁷

PRACTICE

Call-and-Response

CD Track 26 has call-and-response patterns to help you get comfortable with the scale for the IV⁷ chord in concert B♭ blues.

Practice singing with the CD. Then **play** the call-and-response patterns until they are easy for you.

The **3rd-to-7th interchange** is a way of playing the blues by emphasizing the third note of the scale, which as you know, is ½ step lower for the IV⁷ chord (E♭⁷) then it is for the I⁷ chord (B♭⁷). The best way to begin practicing the 3rd-to-7th interchange is by using use the first three notes of the scale.

④ PLAY

Follow the hand signs below to practice the first three notes of the scale for the 3rd-to-7th interchange.

⑤ IMPROVISE

Track 27

Call-and-Response
CD Track 27 features call-and-response melodies to the concert B♭ blues progression, but the melodies are concentrating only on the 3rd-to-7th interchange between the I⁷ and IV⁷ chords. *Therefore, there will be no melodies to imitate when you hear the V⁷ chord.*

Sing and then **play** in response to the CD until you are comfortable imitating the notes and have mastered the 3rd-to-7th interchange. After you have practiced with CD Track 27, you will begin to hear when the progression goes to the IV chord. You are **playing by ear** which is one of the most important aspects to being an improviser!

Track 28

Call-and-Response
CD Track 28 has call-and-response patterns to the blues progression which use the entire scales for the I⁷ (B♭⁷) and IV⁷ (E♭⁷) chords. It should be easy for you to go back and forth between these two scales, since the 3rd is the only different note between the two.

⑥ RECOGNIZE

Track 27

Recognizing Melodies
Circle the two melodies below that are played during the first 24 bars of CD Track 27. **Write** the Roman numerals for the chords they outline.

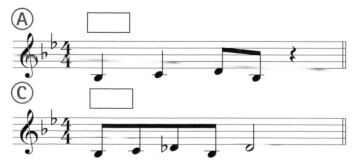

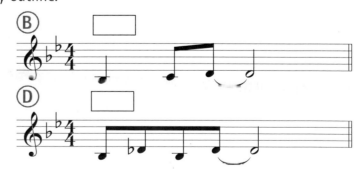

CHOP-MONSTER CHALLENGE 15

Practice playing songs you already know by ear. Begin with "Twinkle, Twinkle Little Star" (start on (B♭). Then try other songs that you know and like. Monster improvisers can play, by ear, any song that they know.

Feeling the Bluesy 3rd

You are now comfortable with the lowered 3rd scale degree that helps **make the change** of the IV chord. (The phrase "make the change" means to play a melody or a melodic note that clearly defines a chord.)

You should also know that this lowered 3rd note may be played over the Tonic (I) chord in the blues, as well. This note is a **blue note**, and could also be called the *flat 3rd, blue 3rd* or the *bluesy 3rd*. The lowered 7th that you play is also a bluesy note, so now you know two blue notes.

When great improvisers use blue notes, they aren't necessarily trying to make the changes, but rather create a bluesy sound that can work with any of the blues chords.

❶ PLAY

Follow the hand signs below to add the flat (blue) 3rd between scale degrees 2 and 3.

Note: You have played flat 3 this way before, as an embellishing chromatic note, briefly passing between 2 and 3. To make this note a blue note, you must emphasize it and give it the blue feeling.

❷ TRANSCRIBE

On the staff below are the roots of the chords for the blues progression. **Notate** the blue 3rd above each root.

❸ PRACTICE

Below are practice patterns that use both the blue 3rd and the blue 7th. As you play them, work to create a bluesy feeling every time you play a blue note. Remember, most of these licks can be played over any of the chords of the concert B♭ blues progression. They don't necessarily define each chord change, but that is not the essential goal of bluesy playing.

④ IMPROVISE

Call-and-Response

CD Track 29 has call-and-response melodies for the concert B♭ blues progression, using the blue 3rd and blue 7th in characteristic ways.

Ⓐ **Practice** singing along, until you can convincingly create a bluesy feeling.

Ⓑ Next, **play** in response to the CD until these bluesy figures are a part of your improvisation vocabulary.

Ⓒ **Listen carefully**! Some of these melodies use the natural 3rd to make the change of the I⁷ chord. It is up to you to hear and imitate these chord tones when they occur.

Ⓓ **Important.** You now understand that both the natural 3rd and the flat 3rd can be consonant for the I⁷ chord in the blues. However, there are two things to remember:

1. It is important to use the natural 3rd when you want to "play the changes."

2. The natural 3rd is only for the I⁷ chord—it sounds very dissonant when played with the IV⁷ chord!

Try It On Your Own!

CD Track 30 is an accompaniment for the concert B♭ blues. Use this track to practice what you've learned so far: scales and chords, 3rd to-7th interchange, and bluesy playing.

> **NOTE:** *A blue 3rd, correctly played, isn't exactly a flatted 3rd, but more likely a note somewhere* **between** *scale degrees 2 and 3. Blue notes convey a feeling of sadness or intensity, and it is this* **feeling** *that creates the bluesy sound.*

CHOP-MONSTER CHALLENGE 16

More Bluesy 3rds

Go back to CD Track 30 and improvise again, this time incorporating the bluesy 3rd above each root of the progression (as you notated them in the Transcribe section of this unit). Notice how your solos sound even more bluesy when you add the other bluesy 3rds.

Mastering the Scale for the V⁷ Chord

In Unit 14 you discovered that the root of the V chord for concert B♭ blues is F.

Improvising to the F⁷ chord will be as easy as the other chords in B♭ blues, because you already know how to do it! The scale that you played in Unit 7 for your Cᴍɪ⁷ chord works just as well for F⁷.

As you recall, that scale is your B♭ major scale, starting and ending on the **second** note of the scale.

❶ PLAY

Follow the hand signs below to play the notes of the concert B♭ major scale as it is used for the V⁷ chord (F⁷).

❷ TRANSCRIBE

(A) **Notate** the scale you just played on the staff below.

(B) **Circle** the note that is the root of the V⁷ chord.

You'll be glad to know that all of the notes of the scale you wrote down—except for one—will be consonant with your F⁷ chord. The only dissonant note is concert B♭. So, all you need to remember is when improvising to a V⁷ chord—the Tonic note is dissonant!

❸ PRACTICE

Below are practice patterns for the scale to the V⁷ chord in concert B♭ blues. You have already practiced this scale, but these patterns are more helpful for creating the sound of the V⁷ chord. **Practice** the patterns until you can improvise with them from memory.

④IMPROVISE

Track 31 **Call-and-Response**
CD Track 31 features call-and-response melodies to the V⁷ chord in concert B♭ blues.

Ⓐ **Sing** in response to the patterns, repeating the track until it feels very comfortable.

Ⓑ Once you are comfortable singing the patterns, **play** in response to the CD.

Track 30 **Try It On Your Own!**
Go back to CD Track 30 and improvise, using the V⁷ patterns you have learned when you hear the V⁷ chord. You should now easily hear when the V⁷ chord rolls around!

⑤RECOGNIZE

Track 32 **Scale Identification**
You have now learned to play scales for each of the three chords in the concert B♭ blues progression. CD Track 32 has short melodies based on these three scales. After each scale melody is played, **circle** the chord symbol below that fits with the scale.

Example 1	Example 2	Example 3	Example 4
B♭⁷ E♭⁷ F⁷	B♭⁷ E♭⁷ F⁷	B♭⁷ E♭⁷ F⁷	B♭⁷ E♭⁷ F⁷

Example 5	Example 6	Example 7	Example 8
B♭⁷ E♭⁷ F⁷	B♭⁷ E♭⁷ F⁷	B♭⁷ E♭⁷ F⁷	B♭⁷ E♭⁷ F⁷

CHOP-MONSTER CHALLENGE 17

For every chord, the 7th of the chord is the note just below the root in the scale that you play. For instance, you know that the 7th of your B♭⁷ chord is A♭, which is the note just before B♭ in the scale.

Ⓐ Your challenge is to find the 7ths of the other chords in the blues progression. On the staff below, **write down** the roots and 7ths of the chords for the B♭ concert blues.

Track 30 **Chop-Monster Practice**

Ⓑ Next, **improvise** to CD Track 30, incorporating all the 7ths you just wrote down (you can use the bluesy 3rds, too).

Ⓒ **Experiment** with how much of a bluesy feeling you can create with these blue notes!

Expanding Your Range

Of course you know that monster improvisers play in more than one octave. You can easily **expand your range** by adding a few notes to the top and bottom of the scales that you know, as the example below shows for the scale for B♭7.

❶ PLAY

Play *all three scales* of the concert E♭7 and F7 blues, adding three notes to the bottom and two notes to the top. First, play from the root down through the extra notes and then back up. Next, start on the root, go up the entire scale including the extra two notes on top, and then come down the entire scale to the root.

❷ TRANSCRIBE

Transcribe the scales for your E♭7 and F7 chords, including the extra notes.

Ⓐ   E♭7

Ⓑ   F7

❸ PRACTICE

Below are a few practice melodies, with expanded range, for each scale in the concert B♭ blues. **Practice** until you can easily play them from memory.

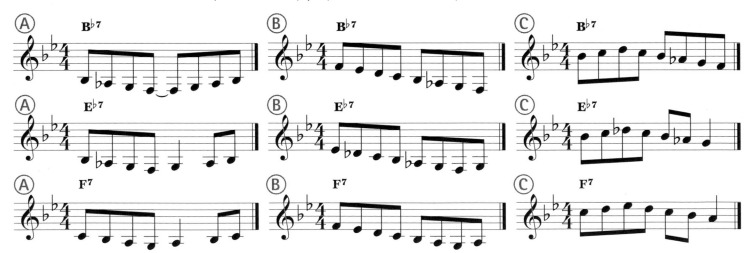

CHOP-MONSTER CHALLENGE 18

Track 33

Call-and-Response

CD Track 33 has call-and-response melodies to the concert B♭ blues progression that add extra notes to the bottom and the top of each of the scales. **Sing** and **play** in response to the CD at least 20 times until you can easily incorporate these ideas into your own improvised solos.

Adding More Chromatic Notes

Monster improvisers are highly adept at using chromatic notes to embellish the consonant notes of the changes. In fact, you learned to use chromatic notes this way in Unit 8. Let's add another chromatic note to your vocabulary.

❶ PLAY

(A) **Follow** the hand signs below to find the chromatic note between the 4th and 5th notes of the concert B♭ major scale.

(B) Next, **play** the first five notes to the scales for your F⁷ and G⁷, adding that exact same pitch.

❷ TRANSCRIBE

Write down the chromatic note as it embellishes the three scales for your B♭ blues:

❸ IMPROVISE

Call-and-Response

CD Track 34 has call-and-response melodies for the concert B♭ blues, incorporating the chromatic note you just learned.

(A) **Sing** in response to the CD, being careful to incorporate the inflection and mood created with the extra note.

(B) Once you are comfortable singing these melodies, **play** in response to the CD until you can use these ideas in your own solos.

CHOP-MONSTER CHALLENGE 19

Try It On Your Own!

A chromatic scale is written on the stave below. Your challenge is to **improvise** to the concert B♭ blues featured on CD Track 30, using just the chromatic scale. The secrets to doing this musically are:

(A) Always keep your place in the changes.

(B) Stop on, or accent notes in the chords, so that the changes will still be heard.

Putting It All Together

Improvising to the blues is often very impassioned, or emotional. If you think of "That's Cool!" as cool improvising, then "That's Right!" represents **hot** improvising—where rhythms are more pronounced and the tone can have more edge.

❶ GETTING READY

You have developed a large vocabulary for improvising on your own to the concert B♭ blues progression of the song "That's Right!" Now you are ready to put it all together. Once again, the chord change are:

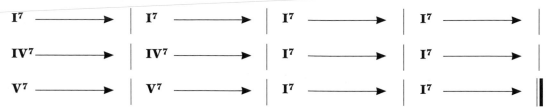

❷ IMPROVISE

Track 35

Call-and-Response
CD Track 35 has call-and-response melodies that are similar to the licks you will play in "That's Right!"

Ⓐ **Sing** in response to the CD, listening carefully to the rhythms and style.

Ⓑ **Play** repeatedly, until each melody feels like your own.

Track 30

Try It On Your Own!
Use CD Track 30 to **improvise** your own solo to the 12-bar blues changes of the song "That's Right!" Incorporate the call-and-response melodies that you have learned.

CHOP-MONSTER CHALLENGE 20

Now you'll have a chance to transcribe another complete solo, this time in the hot style of monster alto-saxophonist Charlie Parker (nicknamed "Yardbird" or "Bird"). He helped to invent the "be-bop" style of jazz which is an essential part of the foundation for all modern jazz improvisation.

Track 36

Transcribe the Solo
CD Track 36 has a solo for you to transcribe to the concert B♭ blues progression. This solo uses melodies that you know, and is played in a style much like that of Charlie Parker.

Ⓐ Find some manuscript paper and a pencil, in case you want to make notes.

Ⓑ **Listen** to CD Track 36 several times before attempting any transcription.

Ⓒ **Review** small sections of the solo, listening to and singing one melody at a time.

Ⓓ **Play** the melodies that you hear, imitating every nuance (subtlety) of inflection.

Ⓔ Once you have it, play along with the alto sax player on CD Track 36. (You can also play the solo to CD Track 30, giving it your own inflection.)

Ⓕ If you can, write down the solo that you have transcribed.

> **LEAVE SPACE WHEN SOLOING:** *Every musical idea must have a beginning and an ending. Think of each phrase you play as a musical sentence. Remember to breathe and leave space before going on to the next sentence. The greatest players in history have left several beats—even several bars—between ideas at certain times!*

Coming to Terms

Write down, in your own words, definitions to each of these jazz terms:

The "Head": _____

Tonic Chord: _____

Dominant Seventh Chord: _____

Mixolydian Scale: _____

12-Bar Blues: _____

Blue Note: _____

Lick: _____

3rd–to–7th Interchange: _____

CHOP-MONSTER CHALLENGE 21

Do some research about Charlie "Yardbird" Parker.

Listen to a recording by Charlie Parker and make four observations about his playing below. (The song "Now's the Time" is a great example of his blues playing.)

Your comments might include a description of his sound or inflection. Make note of the following:

Is his style simple or complex? Is his playing smooth or jagged? Is he passionate or reserved?

1. _____

2. _____

3. _____

4. _____

That's Right!

Shelly Berg

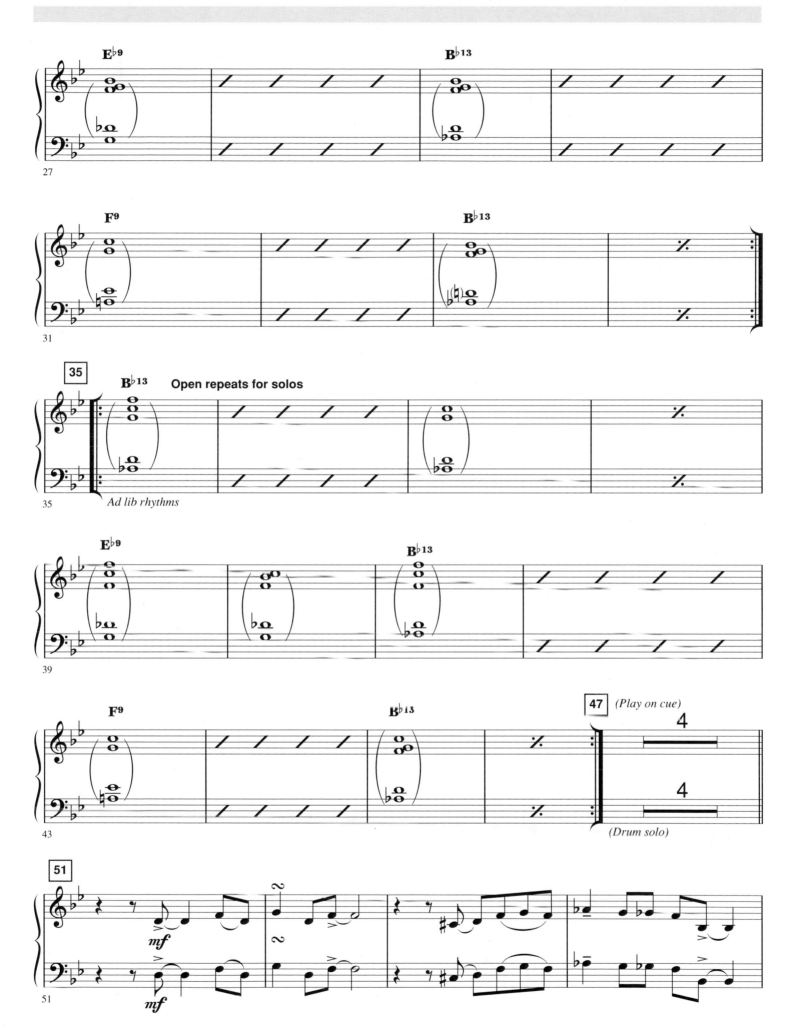

CHOP-MONSTER CHALLENGE 22

Track 37

Big-Band Recording of "That's Right!"
Listen to CD Track 37 several times. As you play "That's Right!," try to imitate the style and articulation of the professional musicians on the recording.

Tips for Blues Comping

Voicing chords with **both hands** adds maturity to your sound (with an expanded range) *and* makes the blues more fun to play! Here's how to get started.

1 Begin by finding chord tones 1 and 5 with your right hand for the I⁷ chord (B♭⁷). Then add the 7th and 3rd in your left hand as shown below.

2 Practice playing your comping rhythms with both hands simultaneously, once again playing off the beat and on the beat. Remember to avoid using the damper pedal and keep your articulations short and crisp.

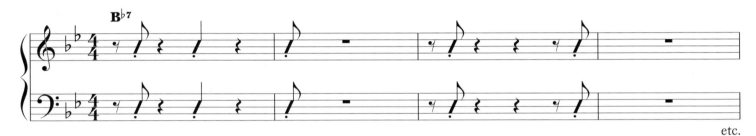

etc.

3 To comp the the IV⁷ chord (E♭⁷), keep the same right hand notes as above. Move your left hand down a ½ step and you'll be playing the 3rd and 7th of the IV⁷ chord*:

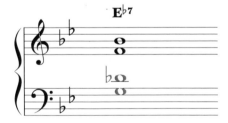

4 Return the I⁷ chord (B♭⁷). Then move your right hand up a whole step, and your left hand up a ½ step, and you're playing the V⁷ chord (F⁷)*!

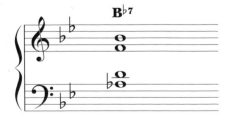
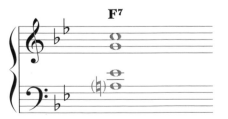

5 Go back to CD Track 30 and practice your comping, using these voicings.

*These chords may sound "extra juicy" to you. That's because they contain a 9th in the voicing you just learned.